SRA Open Court Reading

Beth Gets a Snack

SRA

A Division of The McGraw-Hill Companies

Columbus, Ohio

www.sra4kids.com

SRA/McGraw-Hill

A Division of The **McGraw·Hill** *Companies*

Copyright © 2002 by SRA/McGraw-Hill.

All rights reserved. Except as permitted under the United States Copyright Act, no part of this publication may be reproduced or distributed in any form or by any means, or stored in a database or retrieval system, without prior written permission from the publisher.

Printed in the United States of America.

Send all inquiries to:
SRA/McGraw-Hill
8787 Orion Place
Columbus, OH 43240-4027

ISBN 0-07-569468-9

2 3 4 5 6 7 8 9 DBH 05 04 03 02

Beth is a bug.
Beth is too thin.
Beth wants a snack.

Beth wants fabric for a snack.
But where will Beth get fabric?

This is Seth.
Seth gets a bath.

Seth has a bedspread.
This bedspread has thick red threads.

Beth is thrilled with Seth's bedspread.
Beth has this fabric for a snack!

Seth gets in bed.
Beth is not thin. Beth is fat.
Beth is stuffed with thick red thread!